ISBN 0 86112 790 0
© Brimax Books Ltd 1992. All rights reserved.
Published by Brimax Books Ltd, Newmarket, England 1992.
Printed in France by Pollina, 85400 Luçon (France) - n° 15000

I CAN READ BY
MYSELF

Illustrated by Gill Guile

WHSMITH
EXCLUSIVE
· BOOKS ·

Harvey Rabbit

It is a lovely Spring day. Harvey Rabbit and his friends are spring cleaning their homes.
Harvey Rabbit cleans his burrow.
Olly Owl cleans his nest.
Morris Mouse cleans his hole.
Freddie Frog cleans the leaves from his pond.
Baby Bear helps Mrs Bear to clean their cave.

Harvey Rabbit is in his garden.
He puts his rug over the
washing line. Harvey beats the
rug with his broom. Olly Owl
flies down from his tree.
"What are you doing, Harvey?"
he asks.
"I am cleaning my rug," pants
Harvey.
Dust flies everywhere.

Freddie Frog leaps off his
lily pad.
"What are you doing, Harvey?"
he asks.
"I am cleaning my rug," puffs
Harvey. There is dust
everywhere.
Morris Mouse looks out of
his hole.
"What are you doing, Harvey?"
he asks.
"I AM CLEANING MY RUG!"
says Harvey.

The dust gets into Harvey's eyes. It gets into Morris' nose. It gets into Freddie's mouth. Everyone sneezes while Harvey cleans his rug.
"What are you doing?" asks a very small voice.

15

Harvey and his friends turn around and see a little lamb. They have never seen a lamb before.

"Hello," says Harvey. "Where do you come from?"

"I do not know," says the little lamb. "I am lost."

"We must find your home and take you back," says Harvey. "We will show you our homes. You can tell us if your home is like ours."

Off they go to Harvey's burrow. "Do you live in a burrow like this?" asks Harvey.

The little lamb looks at Harvey's burrow. Then he shakes his head. "Your home is very nice," he says, "but it is not like mine."

"Do you live in a nest?" asks
Olly Owl.
"What is a nest?" asks the little
lamb.
"Come and see," says Olly.
They go to Olly's tree.
Harvey points to Olly's nest up
in the branches.
The lamb looks at Olly's nest.
Then he shakes his head. "Your
home is very nice," he says,
"but it is not like mine."

21

"Do you live in a pond?" asks Freddie Frog.
"What is a pond?" asks the little lamb.
"Come and see," says Freddie. They go to Freddie's pond. Freddie jumps onto his lily pad. The lamb looks at Freddie's pond. Then he shakes his head. "Your home is very nice," he says, "but it is not like mine."

"Do you live in a hole?" asks
Morris.

"What is a hole?" asks the little
lamb.

"Come and see," says Morris.
They go to Morris' hole.
The lamb looks at Morris' round
hole. Then he shakes his head.
"Your home is very nice," he
says, "but it is not like mine."

What can they do now?

"What about my home?" says Baby Bear. He lives in a cave with Mr and Mrs Bear. They all go to the cave.

"Do you live in a cave like this?" asks Baby Bear.

The lamb looks at the cave. Then he shakes his head. "Your home is very nice," he says, "but it is not like mine."

Baby Bear tells Mrs Bear all about their new friend.
"You silly things!" she says.
"This is a lamb! Lambs do not live in burrows or nests or ponds or holes or caves. Lambs live in big green fields."
Mrs Bear tells Olly to fly up into the air to see if he can find any big green fields with other lambs in it.

29

Up flies Olly, into the sky. He can see his friends below. Olly sees the tops of the trees. Then he sees a big green field with some lambs in it, just like their new friend. He flies back to the cave.

"Follow me," he says. "I have found your home, little lamb."

They all follow Olly. Soon they reach the big green field. The lamb sees his mother and runs to her. The lamb's mother is very pleased to see her baby. "Thank you for finding my lamb," she says.

"When I am big," says the lamb, "I will come and play with you again. Goodbye!"

Say these words again

cleaning	lamb
rug	lost
broom	branches
dust	lily
nose	sky
eyes	follow

Where do they live?

burrow

pond

cave

hole

nest

fields

Morris Mouse

One Summer day, Morris Mouse wakes up very early. He can hear lots of funny noises outside. He peeps out of his window.

He can see Sammy Squirrel running up and down his tree. He can see Hoppy Hare jumping high in the air.

He can see Freddie Frog swimming quickly across his pond, and he can see Harvey Rabbit running across the grass.

"What are you all doing?" asks Morris.

"Today is Sports Day," says Sammy, climbing the tree again.

"We are practising," says Hoppy. "I am on Daisy Team. I want to help them win the jumping race."

"And I want to help them win the climbing race," says Sammy.

"I am on Buttercup Team," says Freddie. "And I want to help them win the swimming race."

"And I want to help them win the running race," says Harvey.

"The team who wins gets a big silver cup," says Sammy.

"Which team are you on, Morris?" asks Freddie.

Morris wants to join a team and help win the silver cup. 'I will ask Mr Bear if I can join Daisy Team,' thinks Morris.

Mr Bear is head of Daisy Team. He says Morris can join.

"Thank you," says Morris.

Soon it is time for the first race.
Olly Owl is the judge.
"Everyone get ready to climb
as fast as you can," says Olly.
"Not you, Morris," says
Mr Bear. "Your legs are too
short to climb."
Morris is very sad. He wants to
help Daisy Team.
"Ready, Steady, Go!" cries Olly.
Morris watches his friends
climb. Sammy Squirrel finishes
first. Daisy Team has won.

"Now, get ready to run as fast as you can," says Olly.

"Not you, Morris," says Mr Bear. "You are too slow to run."

Morris is very sad. He wants to help Daisy Team.

"Ready, Steady, Go!" cries Olly. Morris watches his friends run. Harvey Rabbit finishes first. Buttercup team has won this time.

"Now, get ready to swim as fast as you can," says Olly.

"Not you, Morris," says Mr Bear. "Your arms are too short to swim."

Morris is very sad. He wants to help Daisy Team.

"Ready, Steady, Go!" cries Olly. Morris watches his friends swim. Freddie Frog finishes first. Buttercup Team has won again.

"Now, get ready to jump as high as you can," says Olly.
"Not you, Morris," says Mr Bear. "You are too small to jump."
Morris is very sad. He wants to help Daisy Team.
"Ready, Steady, Go!" cries Olly. Morris watches his friends jump. Hoppy Hare jumps highest. Daisy Team has won again.
It is a draw.

The last game is tug-of-war.
"We must win this game, to win the cup," says Mr Bear.
Each team lines up, with a thick rope in the middle.
"Everyone pull as hard as you can," says Olly.
"Not you, Morris," puffs Mr Bear. "You are too small."
Morris is very sad.
"Ready, Steady, Go!" cries Olly. Both teams pull hard. Buttercup Team is winning.

'I must help,' thinks Morris. "Mr Bear," he calls, "please let me pull."

"But you are so small, Morris," pants Mr Bear. "What can you do?"

Morris picks up the end of the rope. He pulls with all his might. Daisy Team is tired, but Morris says, "Come on everyone. We can win. Pull! Pull!"

Buttercup Team laughs when they see Morris. They think he is too small to help. But Morris pulls the rope hard, and makes the rest of the Daisy Team pull hard, too.

Daisy Team pulls and pulls until they win the game.

Daisy Team has won the silver cup!

Mr Bear is very pleased.

Olly Owl presents the silver cup to Daisy Team.
Mr Bear gives it to Morris.
"Well done, Morris," he says.
"I am sorry I did not let you join in all the games. You may be small, but you have helped us to win the cup."

Morris is very proud. He takes the cup home with him that night and he goes to sleep with it beside his bed.

Morris does not feel sad anymore, because he helped Daisy Team win the silver cup!

Say these words again

up	help
down	sad
high	race
win	small
silver	short
judge	rope

What are they doing

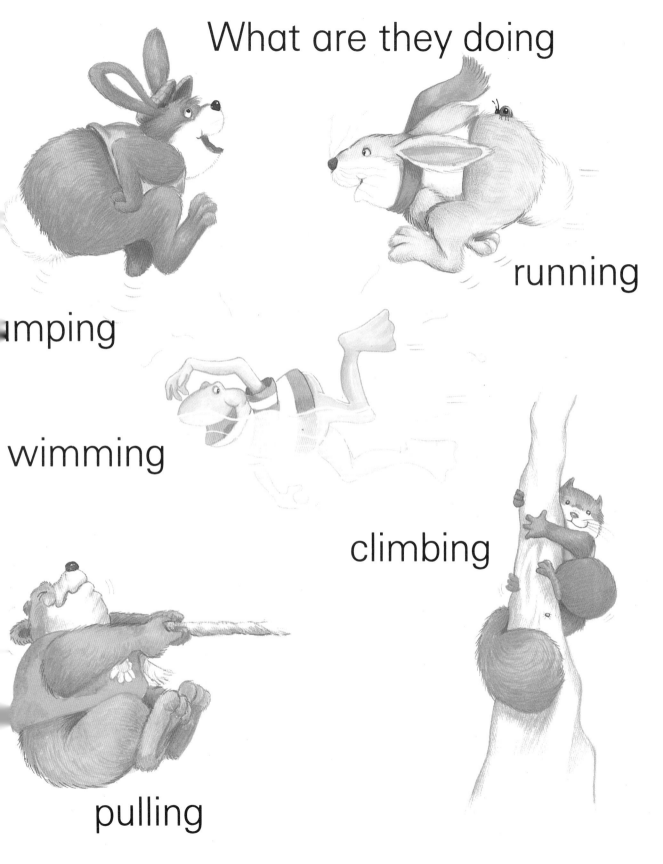

jmping

running

wimming

climbing

pulling

Sammy Squirrel

Sammy Squirrel plays by his hole in the tree.

"Come here, Sammy," says Mrs Squirrel. She gives Sammy a basket. "The leaves are falling from the trees," she says. "Soon there will be no nuts left for us to eat. We must pick lots of nuts to eat during Winter. Go and fill this basket with nuts and bring it home."

Sammy takes the basket. He sets off into the woods. There he sees all his friends. They are looking for good things to eat. They will put the food away to eat in the Winter. They all choose the things they like best. "What will you choose, Harvey Rabbit?" asks Sammy. "Carrots!" says Harvey. "I like carrots best of all."

"What will you choose,
Mrs Mouse?" asks Sammy.
"Blackberries!" says
Mrs Mouse. "I like blackberries
best of all."
"And what will you choose,
Mrs Bear?" ask Sammy.
"Honey!" says Mrs Bear. "I like
honey best of all."
"I like nuts best of all," says
Sammy.

Sammy sees a tall tree. He can
see lots of nuts in the tree.
Sammy takes the basket and
runs up to the top of the tree.
He fills his basket to the brim
with nuts.
"What lovely nuts," he says.
Mrs Squirrel will be pleased
with him.

Below him, Sammy sees Morris Mouse and Baby Bear. "Come and play with us!" they call.

Sammy runs down to join them. He likes to play with his friends. They play hide and seek until Mrs Mouse comes for Morris and Mrs Bear comes for Baby Bear.

"Goodbye," says Sammy as they go.

'It is time for me to go home, too,' thinks Sammy.
But wait! Where is his basket of nuts? Sammy does not know. He has lost it! Oh dear, Mrs Squirrel will not be pleased.
"Where is my basket?" asks Sammy. "I must ask everyone if they have seen it."

Sammy runs to Harvey's burrow.
"Harvey, have you seen my
basket of nuts?" asks Sammy.
"No," says Harvey. "I only have
my carrots and lettuces." He
shows them to Sammy. There
are no nuts there.
"Oh dear!" says Sammy.
"What shall I do now?"
"Have you asked Mrs Mouse if
she has seen your basket?"
says Harvey.

Sammy runs to Mrs Mouse's
hole.
"Mrs Mouse, have you seen
my basket of nuts?" he asks.
"No," says Mrs Mouse. "I only
have my jars of blackberry
jam." She shows them to
Sammy. There are no nuts there.
"Oh dear!" says Sammy.
"What shall I do now?"
"Have you asked Mrs Bear if
she has seen your basket?"
says Mrs Mouse.

Sammy runs to Mrs Bear's cave.

"Mrs Bear, have you seen my basket of nuts?" he asks.

"No," says Mrs Bear. "I only have my jars of honey." She shows them to Sammy. There are no nuts there.

"Oh dear!" says Sammy. "What shall I do now?"

Sammy sits down under a tall tree. He does not want to go home without his basket of nuts. Sammy begins to cry. Then, bop! Something falls from the top of the tree. It falls on Sammy's head.

"Ow!" says Sammy. What can it be? He looks up.

Then, bop! Something falls from the tree again.

"Ow!" says Sammy again. What can it be? Then Sammy sees. This is his nut tree! Nuts are falling from the tree onto his head.

Sammy climbs to the top of the tree. There is his basket! He left the basket in the tree when he went to play with Morris and Baby Bear.

"Hurray!" says Sammy. He takes the basket home to his mother.

"You have worked very hard," says Mrs Squirrel. She is very pleased. "As a treat, you can have some nuts before I put them away."

Sammy eats his nuts. He is very pleased that he has found them again. Now Sammy and Mrs Squirrel will have plenty of nuts to eat during the cold Winter months.

Say these words again

hole	where
leaves	shows
tall	sticky
best	falls
pleased	treat
basket	head

What did they choose?

blackberries

honey

nuts

carrots

Baby Bear

Mrs Bear draws the curtains in the Bears' cave.
Outside it is cold and dark.
"It is Winter now, Baby Bear," she says. "It is time for us to go to sleep."
"But I am not tired," says Baby Bear. "I do not want to sleep."
"Come along, Baby Bear," says Mrs Bear. "Time for bed."
She gives Baby Bear a hot water bottle and tucks him up in bed.

"But I want to go out and play," says Baby Bear.
"All bears go to sleep for the Winter," says Mrs Bear. "We will wake up in the Spring when it is nice and warm. Then you can go out and play."
Mrs Bear puts out the light. She gets into bed. Soon she and Mr Bear are fast asleep.

Baby Bear is still wide awake. He creeps out of bed and looks out of the window. The moon shines on the white frost. It looks like sugar on the trees. Then Baby Bear sees big white flakes of snow falling from the sky. It covers the grass and trees. Baby Bear rubs his eyes. He has never seen snow before. "I hope it is still there in the morning," he says.

Next day, Mr and Mrs Bear are still fast asleep. They will not wake up until the alarm clock rings in the Spring.

Baby Bear jumps out of bed. He runs to the window. The snow is still there! Baby Bear opens the door and goes outside.

"Snow is very cold and wet," says Baby Bear. He makes deep footprints in the snow.

Then Baby Bear sees Harvey
Rabbit and Sammy Squirrel.
They are making snowballs.
Harvey throws a snowball at
Sammy. Thump! It hits Sammy
on the nose. Sammy throws
a snowball at Harvey. Thump!
It hits Harvey on the nose.
"Come and play," they say to
Baby Bear.

Baby Bear makes a snowball and throws it high in the air. "This is fun," says Baby Bear. Thump! His snowball hits him on his head. "Snow is very cold and wet," says Baby Bear, "but I like it!"

They all play in the snow.
Morris Mouse joins in. Olly
Owl flies down from his nest.
"Hoppy Hare is sliding down
the hill," he says. "Come and
play with him."
They all follow Olly to Hoppy's
slide. Hoppy and his friends
slide down the hill.
"Let me try," says Harvey. He
slides down the hill on his
big feet.

"Let me try," says Sammy
Squirrel. He slides down the
hill on his bushy tail.
"Let me try," says Baby Bear.
He has not seen a slide before.
Bump! Baby Bear falls down.
He slides down the hill on his
bottom!
"Snow is very cold and wet,"
says Baby Bear, "but I like it!"

113

"I am going to build a snow rabbit," says Harvey. He starts to make a rabbit out of the snow. "Just like me," he says. "I am going to build a snow squirrel," says Sammy. He starts to make a squirrel with the snow. "Just like me," he says.

"I am going to build a snow mouse," says Morris. He starts to make a mouse with the snow. "Just like me," he says. "I am going to build a snow bear," says Baby Bear. He starts to make a bear with the snow. "Just like me," he says. When the snow animals are finished they look just like the real animals.

Here come Mr and Mrs Bear.
Baby Bear left the door open
and the cold wind woke them
up.
They do not see Baby Bear and
his friends. They only see the
snow animals.
"Look!" says Mrs Bear. "Baby
Bear and his friends are frozen
stiff!" She thinks the snow
bear is Baby Bear.
"Here I am," calls Baby Bear.
"I am not frozen, but I am very
cold and wet."

"I think we should all go home and get warm and dry," smiles Mrs Bear.

In the cave, they all sit by the fire and have toast and honey. Baby Bear tells Mrs Bear all about the snowball fight, and the slide, and the snow animals.

"You have had a busy day,"
says Mrs Bear. "Now will you
go to sleep, Baby Bear?"
Baby Bear does not answer.
Everyone looks at Baby Bear.
He is fast asleep at last!

Say these words again

cold	tired
dark	footprints
frost	fun
white	wet
snow	door
bed	toast

What are they doing

sliding

sleeping

building

throwing

playing